Joseph
Howe

H. R. Percy

Fitzhenry & Whiteside Limited

Contents

The Author

Bill Percy lives in an historic home in Granville Ferry, near
Champlain's Habitation at Port Royal. His short stories have been
published widely and his new novel has won the Nova Scotia
Writers' Award for 1975. Formerly a Lieutenant Commander in
the Royal Canadian Navy, Mr. Percy now devotes his full time
to writing.

©1976 Fitzhenry & Whiteside Limited
150 Lesmill Road
Don Mills, Ontario, M3B 2T5

Printed and bound in Canada.

ISBN 0-88902-220-8

Enchanted Ground Chapter 1

December 13, 1804. Only seven days earlier, in the cathedral of Notre Dame in Paris, Napoleon had arrogantly snatched the crown of France from the hands of the Pope and placed it upon his own head. He was now plotting the invasion of England. On the other side of the Atlantic, President Jefferson of the United States of America was maintaining the uneasy neutrality upon which the fate of the loyal British colonies hung.

For Nova Scotia, these were anxious times. But to those huddled about the hearth of a simple cottage overlooking the Northwest Arm near Halifax, all this must have seemed remote. They had more pressing concerns. It was a night of storm. A gale was howling

The Northwest Arm, Halifax, near the birthplace of Joseph Howe. The tower was built to commemorate the winning of responsible government

John Howe, father of Joseph Howe

What is meant by "Loyalist"?
Who fought the Battle of Bunker Hill? What was the outcome?
Why would it have been necessary for John Howe to leave Boston?

down the Arm, drifting town and country deep in snow. Upstairs in the cottage, remote from all help should anything go wrong, another child was being born.

John Howe, the father, was a pious man, much loved. So doubtless there was prayer. And evidently the prayer was answered: Joseph, a late-comer in a large family, was safely launched upon a life that was to shape the destiny of Nova Scotia and influence the course of history in the colonies that, much against his will, were to become Canada.

In his family and early surroundings the young Joe Howe was fortunate. For the first dozen years, as his poems reveal, he led a life little short of idyllic:

The rod, the gun, the spear, the oar,
I plied by land and sea —
Happy to swim from shore to shore,
Or rove the woodlands free.

He developed in this way a deep love of nature, a contemplative, self-reliant spirit, and the physical and moral resources which the struggles ahead would tax to the limit.

The other children were much older. All but one, his sister Sarah, were by earlier marriages of both parents, but this created no discord. The attachments between them were deep and lifelong. Years after the old cottage had vanished, Joe Howe would sometimes escape from the pressures of his busy life and return with his own sons to drink from the spring that still ran clear; and from the spring of memory, recalling especially his sisters Sarah and Jane and "that venerable patriarch," his father.

John Howe, a printer by trade and an ardent Loyalist, had left his native Boston after the Battle of Bunker Hill, where he had helped tend the wounded. "He left all his household goods and gods, carrying away nothing but his principles and a pretty girl." Those principles were to have a profound effect on the character and conduct of his son Joe. John Howe set up business in Halifax, where in 1791 he founded the *Halifax Journal*. He was a fervent supporter of continuing ties with Britain, and this loyalty combined with his unflagging industry won for him ten years later the posts of King's Printer and Postmaster for the Province of Nova Scotia.

These high-sounding titles brought some prestige and much labour but very little money to support so large a family; and that little he was prone to lavish upon the less fortunate. It was not uncommon for him to take under his roof penniless men in search of work, and to support them until they found it. Joe's mother, a woman "of sterner mood," no doubt disapproved, but John Howe was not to be turned from what he regarded as his duty to his fellow men.

Joe Howe owed most of his early education to his father, a wise and well-read man. Until he was eleven, Joe never went near a school. Then, for two summers, he walked every day three kilometres to school and three kilometres home, disliking every day of it and playing hookey whenever he could. An old lady who had been his schoolmate described him as "a regular dunce; he had a big nose, a big mouth and a big ugly head." But she may well have been prejudiced, for she goes on, "he used to chase me to death on the way home." Under the instruction of his father and his half-sister Jane, at any rate, he was no dunce. Jane, ten years older than Joe, was his "first schoolmistress and pleasant admonisher," while his father later became "my only instructor, my play-fellow, almost my daily companion." Between them they set him fairly on the road to the self-acquired learning that many a college graduate would have later cause to envy. They instilled in him the love of reading and the habit of study that were to make his pen the most powerful in Nova Scotia, his oratory second to none in British North America.

Fare was plain and the cottage was modest, but Joe was to remember his home as standing on "enchanted ground." The property was spacious, for land, at least, was cheap. There were wide lawns bordered with oak trees, while

North the currants formed the hedges,
South the Maples worshipped God.

In spring the whole garden blossomed, and in summer a succession of fruits was there for the picking. The grounds were bounded by a stone wall, but to a child of inquiring mind this was no obstacle. He was soon discovering the many small wonders of the seashore, and roaming the woods where deer and moose were still to be encountered close to home, and where smaller game abounded.

What wars would the old veteran probably have served in, assuming he joined the army about 1755?

For a time an old war veteran — an object no doubt of John Howe's compassion — lived with the family, acting as servant and general handyman. He had travelled widely and was full of strange lore that kindled young Joe's ready imagination, and provided him in later life with many colourful anecdotes and figures of speech. But he imparted practical knowledge, too, teaching the boy to swim in the chilly waters of the Arm, to row, to fish, to box. The boxing was to prove useful, for the youthful Howe was a practical joker whose victims were not always amused.

Every Sunday afternoon John Howe went on foot, Bible under arm, to read and interpret the scriptures to the prisoners of Bridewell. Joe, for many years his father's shadow, soon began to go along. John had a genuine interest in these unfortunate men. When they were released he took them under his care and helped them find work. It was from such encounters, no doubt, that Joe acquired the lively concern for the affairs of ordinary people that was to be one of the great strengths of his political career. But he came to share also his father's disgust at the appalling conditions in the prison, and at the corruption among the governing officials that made those conditions progressively worse. His memory of these abuses was to trigger his eloquence at one of the most critical moments of his adult life.

Returning from one of these excursions to the prison they came one Sunday upon two men fighting as though intent on killing one another. John Howe, who was a magistrate, ordered them to stop. They paused long enough to tell him — not in Sunday language — to mind his own business, and went at it with still greater fury. John, handing the Bible to his son, waded in. He was no longer a young man but, taking each of them by the collar, he banged their heads soundly together, then flung them from him with such force that they fell to the ground ten metres apart. "Now, lads," he said calmly, "let that be a lesson to you not to break the Sabbath in future."

Troubled Thoughts Chapter 2
and Vague Desires

When Joe was thirteen, the state of the family finances
brought an end to his brief schooling, and his real education began in the busy world of his father's print shop
and post office. Often putting in more than fifteen
hours a day, he worked with the other apprentices at
the menial and mechanical tasks of the trade. But in spite
of the heavy work and the long hours, he still had energy
and high spirits left to torment his workmates. In one
instance he carried his pranks so far that his victim left
and, although indentured to Joe's father, went to work
elsewhere.

What is an apprentice?
*Are there still apprentices
today?*
*What is meant by
"indentured"?*

John Howe brought a legal action against the other
printer for the return of his apprentice. The boy having
testified in court to the reason for his departure, young
Joe Howe was called as witness. He more than held his
own under the sarcastic grilling of the defence counsel.
Being asked at last, "And what position do you hold?"
he gave, despite a painful tendency to stammer, an early
example of his gift for repartee: "The same as you seem
to hold here, that of chief devil."

*What would be the duties of
a printer's devil?*

But beneath the playfulness lay a profoundly serious
nature. He soon began to feel the promptings of a "rest-
less, agitating uncertainty." Some high, unknown destiny beckoned him, and he was determined to grasp it.
Joe absorbed avidly all that his father could teach him,
but he found that his only time for quiet thought was
during the long walks to and from work. After a time,
he began staying in Halifax, returning home only for
weekends. In this way, after his gruelling day's work,
he was able to read until 12 or 1 o'clock, and sometimes
even later. "If it were not for my maxim of borrowing
from the night," he told his sister, "my stock of ideas
would receive but precious few additions." His books,
he complained, were few, "but then the world is before
me — a library open to all — from which poverty of
purse cannot exclude me — and in which the meanest

St. Paul's Church and part
of Argyle Street, Halifax, as
they would have been during
Joseph Howe's apprentice
days

and most paltry volume is sure to furnish some thing to
amuse, if not to instruct and improve."

The world before him offered instruction enough.
Halifax was the seat of government, an important garrison, and a busy naval and commercial port. It reflected in
miniature all the activities, fashions and follies of the
great world beyond. On busy days, sailors and soldiers
crowded the streets. German, Dutch, and New England
Loyalist farmers offered their produce for sale. Among
those hurrying about their business were liberated black
slaves from the United States, now in a new bondage of
poverty, selling brooms and wild berries; dispossessed
Micmacs, and the sons and daughters of dispossessed
Acadians, come back to claim some pitiful remnant of
their birthright.

Who were the Acadians?
Where had they come back
from and why had they gone
away in the first place?

Under the guns of the Citadel, sailing ships came and
went, and horse-drawn wagons fetched and carried away
their cargoes. Along the waterfront, ships in all stages of
construction rested on their slips or sprouted new masts
and rigging at their fitting-out berths. From sailmakers'

lofts, shipwrights' shops and smithies came the sounds of thriving industry, and smells of canvas, wood, hot iron and pitch to mingle with those of the lively trade in fish. In dockside taverns, voices in a variety of languages quarrelled and sang. And aloof from all this, the members of "society" paraded in their carriages and fine clothes, the young ladies lowering their eyes and blushing at the gallantries of the strutting officers in their splendid uniforms.

The Halifax scene gave young Howe much food for thought. "What a book I could write if I were to go about sketching its queer old streets and snug interiors, in the spirit of Dickens," he was to write later. But the social critic was already awake in him, and when he did write of Halifax society, his pen was often dipped in gall.

If his books were few, he somehow managed during these years to cover an astonishing range in his reading. This hard-won learning would be reflected later in his writing and his speeches in the form of ready quotation and apt allusion. It was inevitable that he should begin to write. His first poem was published when he was sixteen. Its title, not surprisingly, was "My Father." Then after a feverish burst of composition, he began a three-year "warfare with the muses," avoiding works of the imagination and refraining from "the sin of rhyme." But by 1825 he had made peace with the muses, and the publication of his long poem "Melville Island" in the *Novascotian* won extravagant praise.

Since the poem pleased and impressed the lieutenant-governor, it won for Howe an entrée of sorts into the polite society whose mecca was Government House. A brilliant literary career, it must have seemed, lay before him. "Poetry was the maiden I loved," he was to declare, looking back on all this, "but politics was the harridan I married." As it turned out, the harridan (or horrible old woman) was probably kinder to him than the maiden would have been. Although he revived the love affair with poetry at intervals in later life, almost all his verse was strangled to death by rigidity of form and the current ideas of what was "poetic."

His restlessness was increasing. "If I could be content to go along quietly and peaceably like my neighbours and at the end of some fifty or sixty years tumble into my grave and be dust, I should be happy." But the "infernal feeling" of his high destiny drove him on. At 22, he longed for wider scope and hankered after "the glorious privilege of being independent" in matters of expression. Although his future was obscure, he sensed that freedom of the pen was to figure largely in it. His father's business, tied as it was to government patronage, allowed no such freedom. "We can never take the popular side," Joe complained, "in anything that is going forward."

There were long months of indecision about his future. His father's business went as a matter of course to Joe's elder half-brother John. There would never be enough income from it to support two families. Joe thought seriously of studying law but was deterred by the "chicane and unprincipled petty foggery of the profession." His low regard for lawyers was modified as a result of his later friendship with many eminent barristers, but he never completely abandoned it. This opinion helped to shape his politics, and since lawyers dominated the political scene it would get him into several scrapes over the years.

John Howe, Junior, half-brother of Joseph Howe

For a time he was fired by the idea of going to South America. His sister Sarah's husband, who held a good position in England, was transferred to Peru. To Joe, this seemed like a call to go forth and conquer the world. His parents were opposed to the scheme, but Joe could be persuasive. Soon it was agreed that he should go to join Sarah in Lima. Having acquired a good reading knowledge of French, he now began to teach himself Spanish. But he was never to see Peru. Before his plans were complete, Sarah died at sea, and was buried in Virginia.

Early in 1827, Howe took the first decisive step. In partnership with James Spike, he purchased a weekly newspaper and began publishing it as the *Acadian*, while still devoting most of his time to his father's business. And about this time, Joe's glowing vision of the future was intensified by his meeting with Catherine Susan Ann McNab, who was to become in a very short time

> the guiding star whose living beam
> Flashed o'er youth's troubled thoughts and vague desires.

Although Howe was driving himself harder than ever he found time most evenings to row out to McNab's Island (named for Susan Ann's grandfather), which commanded the harbour entrance. The daughter of an army captain,

Susan Ann was born in 1807 at the barracks in St. John's, Newfoundland. The family soon afterwards moved to McNab's Island where, comparatively isolated in the midst of all the exciting comings and goings of the busy seaport, she grew up.

No doubt she was there watching with her parents on that memorable day during the War of 1812 when the British frigate *Shannon*, having avenged a long series of naval defeats by capturing the United States ship *Chesapeake*, sailed proudly into Halifax with her prize. It was a Sunday, and excitement ran so high that a minister was deserted in mid-sermon by his congregation when they fled down to the harbour to cheer the *Shannon* alongside.

The man who won the heart of Susan Ann was clearly not the dunce with a big, ugly head remembered by the old lady. Speaking of Howe's brothers William and John, a contemporary writes that they were "two most splendid specimens of men, tall, of great physique, altogther fine looking," and he goes on, "as were David and Joseph."

Halifax as Howe would have seen it from McNab's Island during his courtship of Susan Ann McNab

Why was the War of 1812 fought between Britain and the United States?
How did this war affect the British colonies in North America?

The earliest surviving portrait of Howe confirms the
largeness of the nose (but not its ugliness), and shows
him with beetling brows, a strong mouth and a firm
chin. Of Susan Ann's appearance at this time there is no
record, beyond Howe's poetic reference to her "hazel
eye" and "placid smile," but it is safe to assume that Joe
Howe did not row several kilometres every day to court
a plain woman, even though she was "possessed of a
vigorous mind and much good sense."

Love of Susan Ann, at any rate, "fed Ambition's fierce
but smothered fires," and by the end of 1827, Joe Howe
was already chafing against the limitations of the
Acadian. A four-page weekly offered little scope and
James Spike had none of Howe's ambition. In December,
Howe sold out to Spike, and on 1 January, 1828 took over
the *Novascotian*. To many it must have seemed a gamble.
The paper's circulation was not great, and was expected
to diminish with the arrival of a new, little-known editor.
But Howe himself had so few qualms that exactly a
month after his first issue was published, he and Susan
Ann were married. "Having some trust in Providence,"
he wrote, "and . . . a modest reliance on my own head and
hands, I saddled myself with a wife and obligation to
pay £1050 or £210 a year for five years, and went to work
to feed and clothe the former and to fulfil the latter as
fast as I could."

Although he had still a naive faith in the system of
government and the social institutions under which he
lived, Howe staked out his editorial territory very clearly
from the outset:

"While we were connected with the *Acadian*, by far the greater
portion of our time was devoted to a Government Office, which,
although we never allowed it to bias our opinions, to warp our
judgments, or restrain our pen, left us open to imputations, which
strike at the very foundations of an editor's usefulness . . . .
We now stand free of every connection — beyond the influence of
Government — and we trust above the suspicions of the people
. . . . We are no cold approvers, but ardent admirers of the system
under which we live . . . . But the Press, like a two-edged Sword,
waving round the Constitutional Tree, should defend it alike from
the misguided zeal of the People, and the dangerous encroachment
of the Rulers; . . . we will therefore as steadily defend the Government when its acts are just, as we will boldly warn the People when
they are unjust . . ."

These words foreshadowed much of Joe Howe's
future career.

Just Plain Joe: Chapter 3
The Reformer Wakes

In the summer of 1828, to enroll new subscribers and collect money, Joe Howe travelled around western Nova Scotia. He went mostly on horseback, for the roads were primitive. To reach the more remote farms and hamlets he sometimes journeyed whole days on foot, often with little result. "I send you a few pounds," he wrote despondently to Susan Ann, who with the help of Joe's father was producing the paper in his absence, "and am sorry they are so few but really I fared worse at Liverpool than at Lunenburg, scarcely collecting sufficient to pay my expenses."

But if his travels were arduous and not always profitable, they were rich in experience and insight. As he plodded from farm to country inn, Joe Howe was getting to know the people and the people were getting to know him. He was as welcome in the humblest fisherman's shack as in the finest mansion. The arrival of this big energetic young man, full of heartiness and good humour, was an event to be remembered. Many years later, when to city folk he was The Honourable Joseph Howe or Mr. Premier, he was proud to claim that to the farmers and fishermen he was still plain Joe Howe. Coming ravenous to their tables after a hard day on the road, he would do flattering justice to the farm wives' cooking, and in return would treat the family to all the latest news, and enliven their evening with his ready if not always delicate wit. He was not averse to a mild flirtation, either. A young girl boasted to her friends: "Joe Howe came to our house last night. He kissed Mamma and he kissed me too."

As a result of his travels, he published in the *Nova-scotian* a series of essays entitled "Western Rambles"

Geldert's Inn, Windsor, one of the places Joseph Howe stayed during his travels in western Nova Scotia

and, later, "Eastern Rambles." These, with his letters to Susan Ann, reveal a great deal about Howe's character and show this as a vital, formative period of his career. Unwittingly, by being "just plain Joe Howe," he was sowing the seeds of his future popularity and power. He emerges as a man of apparent contradictions, full of love and compassion for simple folk but swift to scold them for their follies; identifying with them, yet burning with the conviction of his own capacity for greatness. The refinement of his writing, and later of his oratory, contrasted strongly with his occasional coarseness of speech. As when, referring to the continual carping criticism of his opponents, he said in the House of Assembly, "I turn my duff to those gadflies." His detractors made much of this coarseness. When he was with rough folk he paid them the compliment of speaking as they spoke, but when he used coarse speech elsewhere it was probably to mock the empty sham of social refinement.

Howe frequently criticized the city dwellers, and the country folk for aping them. While portraying farm life as idyllic, he rebuked the farmers for their tendency to idleness, their families' vanity in dress, their taste for alien luxuries. He was not, however, above enjoying those luxuries himself. Having praised a wayside inn that offered " a good cup of tea, a hot johnny cake, and excellent butter," it did not strike him as odd that he should admonish the farmers: ". . . if you must have tea, go and gather some leaves from the hillside and the good woman will make some for you; but as to bringing a weed from China to fatten a Ploughman in Nova Scotia, there never was a more confounded Humbug."

But compassion was always present. In one letter to his wife he tells how "I fell in with a decent shoemaker from New Brunswick in search of employ — and he having strained the cords of his leg in his travels I made him mount my nag and was thus enabled to help him some miles on his journey while I played pedestrian by the aid of his walking stick." Old John Howe's example was still at work.

During Howe's travels he had much time to indulge his love of nature, and much time for thought. He often went out of his way to visit a waterfall or a lake, or to get a good view from a hilltop. He exclaimed over the beauties of the countryside and the charms of the small towns

Why do you suppose Howe would consider vanity in dress and a taste for luxury to be harmful to the farming families?

Ross farmhouse

Ross Farm, Lunenburg County, Nova Scotia, where Howe would probably have been invited to stay during his "rambles"

that seemed to grow out of rather than to despoil the landscape. But in this, as in so much else, he had vision ahead of his time. Alternating with his pleasure at the spread of cultivation and the growing prosperity of his native province, was a recurring sadness at the impossibility of finding "a scene of any extent into which man, with his devastating improvements, has not intruded." Out of his meditations on the lonely road came equally strong and advanced views on religious and racial tolerance, the dignity of the common man, and the conservation of wild life. Yes, and on the place of women in society: "And now, my fair countrywomen . . . I cannot refrain from asking whether you think nature intended you for nothing better than lacing your stays, and curling your hair. . . . Were woman formed to 'suckle fools and chronicle small beer' or were they formed for higher and nobler purposes?"

How do you explain the apparently contradictory phrase "devastating improvements"?
How have subsequent events justified Howe's uneasiness on this subject?

Such opinions, together with his growing awareness as he went about the province that all was far from well with the system by which the people were governed, were slowly converting the young Howe, Tory by tradition, into an ardent reformer.

Joseph Howe's desk

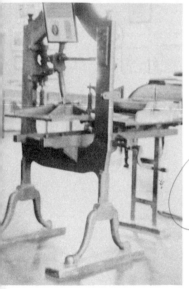

Printing press used by Howe

When at home he continued to work and play at an incredible pace. In addition to his normal newspaper work, he published during this period Thomas Chandler Haliburton's *Historical and Statistical Account of Nova Scotia* and several other works. He wrote at this time in favour of a Mechanics' Institute, which he later took a leading part in forming, chiefly for educational purposes. Shut up in his office, sometimes for days on end, Howe studied newspapers and political writings from other countries, and prepared articles and editorials. Then perhaps he would emerge at midnight to run down to the Market Slip and plunge into the harbour for a swim. Sometimes he would "relax" by spending an afternoon at racquets with his brother William. Joe was able to hold his own, even though William was reputed to be the best player in the colonies.

From 1829 to 1836, Howe's writings became increasingly political. In July 1829 he formed a one-man press gallery in the House of Assembly, and began publishing a long series of "Legislative Reviews." This activity was frowned upon by many members, who tried to stop it; but Howe, jostled in the public gallery, using his hat for a desk, persisted. It was all part of a scheme — pursued with a sure instinct, if as yet with no clear idea of an ultimate purpose — for the political education of the people of Nova Scotia. Howe rightly claimed that without these "reviews," the voters would be as ignorant of the doings of their representatives "as if they had assembled on the moon." Steeped in the British parliamentary tradition, he knew that informed public opinion was the only defence against abuse of power.

The government consisted of the lieutenant-governor representing the king; an Executive Council of twelve appointed members; and the House of Assembly elected by the freeholders of the province. At first, Howe had championed the Council, seeing it as a body of wise and well-intentioned men. Very soon, however, he realized that it had unbridled power which it sometimes used in shameful ways. The Council appointed judges and public officials (and had a good proportion of these within its ranks), and bought their loyalty with handsome salaries, but the Assembly had to find money to pay them by taxing its electors. When the Assembly tried to oppose the Council, as it did in 1830 over a question of the duty to be imposed on brandy, the Council had a simple solution. By refusing to pass one minor item in the Revenue Bills it blocked the passage of all legislation, effectively halting government business and forcing a general election.

Thus began in earnest the long fight for responsible government in Nova Scotia, and Joe Howe in his role as political commentator plunged in with a will. Largely as a result of his efforts, all but one of the candidates favouring reform were elected. After the bitterness of the struggle, much was hoped of this new Assembly. It was expected to work for changes in the composition of the Council; reduction in government spending; currency reform; and the admission of the public to Council meetings, over which, said Howe, "the secrecy of the Inquisition still hangs."

What is "responsible government"? Why would Howe consider it so superior to the existing system?

The House of Assembly, Province House, Halifax. The Speaker's chair is in the centre, with Howe's portrait on its right. This picture was taken from the gallery where Howe made notes "on the crown of his hat" for his "Legislative Reviews"

But three years later, so little had been done that Howe exploded into print with: "Though some of you were steeped to the lips in pledges, you have moved no resolution, offered no address, provoked no debate; but, like the Gladiator of old, have become suddenly awed by or enamoured of the monster we sent you to slay." In 1834, without consulting the Assembly, the Council made a large increase in the Civil List (the money used to pay its officials) and scornfully rejected the Assembly's protests. After much discussion, angry members proposed resolutions aimed at changing the constitution of the Council, but since the House was divided on the issue these attempts were easily foiled.

Using the growing power of his pen, Howe was emerging ever more clearly as the champion of the people, but as his language became less and less restrained he was also making enemies in high places. These enemies awaited their chance, and when in 1835 it seemed Joe Howe had overstepped himself, they were quick to spring the trap.

Joseph Howe, about 1834

A Time of Trial Chapter 4

On the first day of 1835, Howe published a letter written
by his friend George Thompson and signed "The People,"
which accused the magistrates and police of Halifax of
grievous and long-standing misconduct. It attacked the
excessive and unjustly shared burden of taxation and the
misuse of public money over a period of 30 years, and
alleged that "the affairs of the county have been for
years conducted in a slovenly, extravagant and unpopular
manner." It spoke of "a young and poor country . . .
where the many must toil to support the extortions and
exactions of the few; where the hard earnings of the
people are lavished on an Aristocracy, who repay their
ill timed generosity with contempt and insult . . . "

Howe well knew the seriousness of the step he had
taken. Only a few years before, another Halifax editor
had been jailed for two years for a similar "offence,"
and when a charge of libel was brought against Howe
there were many who believed he would suffer a similar
fate. Having asked several lawyers if they thought his
case was defensible and having been assured that it was
not, "I asked them to lend me their books, gathered an
an armful, threw myself on a sofa, and read libel law
for a week. By that time I had convinced myself that they
were wrong, and that there was a good defence. . . ." He
courageously undertook to defend himself, before a chief
justice he had used roughly in print and barristers whose
profession he had frequently criticized.

What is libel?
How does it differ from slander?

Not until late on the night before the trial did he
decide that he had done everything possible, "having
only had time to commit to memory the two opening
paragraphs of the speech. All the rest was to be im-
provised as I went along." Then he put it all aside and
went for a long walk with Susan Ann who, as was written
of her many years later, "stood beside him as his stay
and comforter, with words of cheer and consolation,
always making the best out of the worst features of the
trouble." Both had need of her cheerfulness. Howe was
already burdened with the debts that would plague him
for most of his life. The birth of their third child was

imminent. The first had died when only a few days old. The second, Helen, was now four. What would become of the family if Howe went to prison, or if Susan Ann did not survive the birth? — a possibility not to be lightly dismissed in those days. But, he told her that night in the midst of all these forebodings, if only everything that had gone into his head would only come out, he was sure to win.

The next morning, however, he was still "harassed by doubts and fears" until he saw the effect of his opening words on the jury. "I was much cheered," he wrote, "when I saw the tears rolling down one old gentleman's cheek. I thought he would not convict me if he could help it." As a boy, Howe had stammered badly, but now, sensing his power, he spoke with growing assurance. In the words of the *Acadian Recorder* (7 March, 1835): "Mr. Howe pled his own cause and in a speech of six hours, distinguished by great ability and sparkling eloquence, brought to light a mass of abuses which are without parallel, and which astonished the audience. Innumerable complaints were before current and in everybody's mouth . . . these he collected . . . and brought to bear on his argument with irresistible effect, set them off with so many happy strokes of wit, and in language so brilliant and energetic, as to carry conviction to every mind . . . "

Among the "mass of abuses" were those Howe and his father had witnessed years before in Bridewell prison, which had continued and grown worse in the interval. "I can recall a period when my father interested himself deeply for the welfare of the poor inmates of that prison," Howe told the court. He added pointedly: "Though a magistrate himself, I mention his name with veneration . . . he never filched from them their daily bread, but he sought to impart to them the bread of life . . . he had nothing to do with [the other magistrates'] dirty accounts and paltry peculations." He described how his father had left the place in disgust and had never been back since.

Howe said he could prove that Commissioner Roach and his hirelings were literally "filching the daily bread" of the prisoners, diverting prison funds to their own use, and using the labour of convicts for their private purposes. "Even the melody of Miss Roach's canaries was breathed through cages manufactured at the public expense."

If he were found guilty, Howe told the jury, they should send him to prison, but not to Bridewell. "If you send me there, I shall be compelled to print him a newspaper for nothing and then the list of his luxuries will be pretty complete."

In contrast to all this fraudulent luxury, he told of a prisoner who was forced to wear a spiked dog collar for some trivial offence, and of a woman left in the stocks all night for refusing to yield to the desires of a prison guard. He told the story of a Miss Hogg, who had been awarded £200 when her house was pulled down to prevent the spread of fire. Many months later, with nearly half the award still unpaid, she was arrested for being £2 in arrears with her taxes. It is small wonder that, as Howe cited one example after another, "The defendant was frequently interrupted by expressions of popular feeling."

Howe pointed out that the court was only to consider his motives in printing the letter, and could not call evidence on the truth or falsehood of the charges the letter contained. Thus, by bringing action against him, his accusers had secured themselves against investigation. "Why," Howe demanded, "have they not afforded the means indispensable to a calm and enlightened review of their public conduct? Gentlemen, they dared not do it. They know that . . . it might be safer to attempt to punish me than to justify themselves. There is a certain part of a ship through which when a seaman crawls, he subjects himself to the derision of the deck, because it is taken as an admission of cowardice and incompetence; and had not these jobbing justices crawled in here through this legal lubber hole of indictment, I would have sent them out of court in a worse condition than Falstaff's ragged regiment." Laughter and applause were suppressed by court officers.

"Were I only concerned," Howe declared as the trial drew near its end, "I would not fatigue you further at this late hour, but the principles to be fixed by your verdict will be important to your children and mine." And again: "The press has constantly vindicated and maintained the independence of juries; English juries have been the steady friends and protectors of the press; and I now commit myself and the press of Nova Scotia to your keeping . . . "

After retiring for only ten minutes, the jury brought in its verdict of "Not guilty." It was received with wild applause that spread immediately to the crowds outside. Howe was "borne by the populace to his home, amid deafening acclamations. The people kept holiday that day and the next. Musical parties paraded the streets at night. All the sleds in town were turned out in procession, with banners; and all ranks and classes seemed to join in felicitation on the triumph of the press."

Susan Ann, five days after the trial, gave birth to a healthy boy.

Howe being borne on the shoulders of the crowd after his acquittal in the trial for libel

40304

Chapter 5 "I Will Endeavour to be a Man"

Haliburton owes his chief claim to fame to the invention of a fictional character. What was the name and profession of this character?

Howe was riding high. "In one leap and bound in the course of a single year," wrote his friend George Fenety, "he cleared all obstacles and became the most prominent man and the loudest talked of in all Nova Scotia." His friends and admirers urged him with increasing insistence to seek election to the Legislature. The one exception was Thomas Chandler Haliburton, whose friend and publisher he continued to be. If he ran for election, warned Haliburton, the *Novascotian* would no longer be considered independent, and both Howe and the paper would suffer.

But the call of destiny was clear. Much as he had done to educate and rally the people, Howe now saw that until there was a majority of determined reformers in the House, with strong leadership, the old abuses would continue. Accordingly, he ran as candidate for the County of Halifax, and on his thirty-second birthday, December 13, 1836, he was elected. In the midst of the popular rejoicing at his victory, he was sobered by the death of his father. His sense of loss was profound, and frequently throughout his career he would pay tribute to John Howe and acknowledge his influence. "He left me nothing but his example and the memory of his many virtues, for all that he ever had was given to the poor." And no doubt those "many virtues" were very much present to the newly elected Assemblyman when he said to his electors: "Pardon me if, in this moment of triumph . . . I am but a child; in the scenes of intellectual contention which await me; in those struggles for your rights and interests which are yet to come, I will by the blessing of God, endeavour to be a man."

It was no child who, on the very day the new Assembly was sworn in, plunged into the fight with a resolution stating: "this House recognizes no religious distinctions, and is bound to extend not only equal justice, but equal courtesy, to all." On that same day he seconded a series of resolutions calling upon the Council to open its meetings to the public, and on that issue made his maiden speech. The people, he said, were indignant that the Council should "sit in secret conclave to transact the public business." He termed it an insult to the people, and commented that even the British House of Lords would not dare close its doors to the public. The resolutions were passed unanimously. The Council responded by telling the Assembly to mind its own business. The Council would conduct it affairs as it saw fit.

The long battle was on. The week after the Council's contemptuous reply, two resolutions designed to avoid a head-on clash with the Council were brought before the House. Howe was quick to recognize the danger of appeasement. One such surrender and the new House would be in the same powerless position as the old. He therefore moved, in "amendment," ten resolutions of his own. These summarized all the "evils arising from the imperfect structure of the upper branch" which, instead of reflecting the regions and the varied interests of the province, was composed of residents of Halifax, mostly paid government servants.

The Council was riddled with family and business connections. Ignorant of the needs of the outlying regions, it consistently thwarted the efforts of their elected representatives. It blocked all attempts to reduce excessive salaries and to abolish useless positions; to liberalize education; to extend foreign trade to ports other than Halifax; to abolish illegal fees imposed by Supreme Court judges. It denied the right of the Assembly to decide how tax money raised in the province should be spent. There was flagrant religious discrimination in the structure of the Council, and this was carried down through all levels of the public service. The chief justice, instead of being clearly impartial as his job required, was publicly regarded as a party leader in the Council. Howe's resolutions raised again the question of public admittance to meetings of the Council, and proposed that the upper house be reformed to make it more responsible to the people. It was proposed that these and other complaints be embodied in an address to His Majesty.

What are the functions of a chief justice? Why was it undesirable that he should be a party leader?

Preoccupied though he was with thoughts of his dying mother, Howe made lengthy speeches in defence of these resolutions. In the ensuing debate, which lasted three weeks, the new member found himself pitted against the "big guns" of the government party, including James Boyle Uniacke, the government leader. Howe more than held his own, however, and all the resolutions passed easily. The response should have been foreseen, but when it came three days later it threw the Assembly into a state of panic. The upper house, singling out the phrase "Members of His Majesty's Council have evinced a disposition to protect their own interests and emoluments [salaries] at the expense of the public," demanded the withdrawal of the resolution in which it occurred. The Council threatened to resort to its old blackmailing tactics of holding up the revenue bills and thus paralyzing all business until its demand was met. To many it looked as though Howe's political career was coming to an early and inglorious end. He seemed to have no course but retreat and exposure to public ridicule.

Late the next day, Howe took his place, broadly smiling, and in a few words explained his plan. The House, he said, should not only oblige the Council by withdrawing the offending resolution, but should withdraw them all. They had done their work. They would be studied by the people of Nova Scotia and they would be sent to the British government. By its conduct, the Council was committing the very abuse of which the resolutions complained, and so had publicly condemned itself. Howe proposed that the Assembly prepare an address to the Crown on the state of the province, to be introduced after the revenue bill had been safely passed. This address, containing the substance of all the original resolutions, was passed by the House two weeks after the passage of the bills. This triumph greatly increased Howe's prestige. Less than three months after entering the Assembly, he had become its most powerful force.

Throughout his battle for reform, Howe often affirmed his loyalty to the British Empire, and from first to last he asked only for "what exists at home" (that is, in England). For many years he had an almost naive faith in the fairness and effectiveness of British colonial policy. In the end, this faith was to be severely shaken.

By this time, rebellion was brewing in Upper and Lower Canada (Ontario and Quebec). In 1835, Howe had received two letters from the Lower Canadian radical H. S. Chapman, asking for the support of Nova Scotia's

What was the rebellion in Canada all about? Who were its leaders?

reformers. But Howe shrewdly foresaw that the Canadas were headed for armed rebellion against Britain, and his reply made clear that he wanted no part of it. When the rebellion did break out in 1837, opponents of reform in Nova Scotia were quick to spread the idea that armed violence was the inevitable result of any attempt to secure constitutional changes. Publication of Chapman's letters and Howe's reply effectively silenced this criticism and won favour for Howe in British government circles.

Chapter 6 **Responsible Government: A Trial of Strength**

In August 1837, two dispatches arrived from Lord Glenelg, the British Colonial Secretary, in reply to the Assembly's resolutions and address. They were cordial in tone and gave ungrudging approval to most of the reforms proposed. But the contents of these dispatches were not revealed to the House until the end of the following January.

During the interval, the Council did all in its power to thwart Lord Glenelg's good intentions. For example, the dispatches approved the separation of the Council into a legislative and an executive branch, a compromise that had earlier been reluctantly accepted by Howe in place of a fully elected Council. This meant that the members of the executive branch would still be appointed, not elected.

Influenced by the Council, Lieutenant-Governor Sir Colin Campbell sent for Howe. He did not offer to show him the dispatches but he said he thought that the out-lying parts of the province could not supply enough able men to form two councils. Howe disposed of this shallow argument by writing down at once enough names for both branches. His "rambles" had not been in vain. Sir Colin was noncommital, observing only that Howe had not included his own name.

When the names of the new members of Council were at last announced, it was obvious that no real gains had been made. The new Executive Council was packed with men who could be counted upon to continue the old abuses; while out of a Legislative Council of nineteen, only one, Herbert Huntington, supported the cause of reform. Not long afterwards, taking advantage of con-fused instructions issued by the governor-general, the government reduced and reconstituted both Councils. Huntington lost his seat and the governing clique was

more firmly in power than ever. Against the clear instructions of Lord Glenelg, both Councils were heavily
weighted in favour of the Church of England, which represented only one-fifth of the population.

The Colonial Secretary had also agreed that the
Assembly should have the right to control the spending
of its own tax revenues, and assume responsibility for
establishing and paying the salaries of government
officers. Huntington prepared a Civil List Bill for this
purpose. It was more generous to the office-holders than
Howe and his supporters thought they deserved, but
when the Bill came before the Council it was swiftly rejected.

These and many other frustrations led to the drafting
of a second address to the Crown, but this brought a
series of dispatches from England that, in effect, can-
celled all the concessions made the year before. The
Assembly decided to send a delegation to London. It
was obvious, said Howe, that the Colonial Office was
being influenced by persons with an interest in maintaining the corrupt system in Nova Scotia. "When an office
becomes vacant, home go a sheaf of gentlemen to seek
for it." This back-door diplomacy was so widespread
that there was "hardly a public servant in the Province,
who could not, by his representation and influence,
thwart any resolution or address which the assembled
representatives of the whole country thought it their
duty to adopt." Howe, by this time a shrewd politician,
publicly supported the delegation but declined to join it.
He knew that his enemies would take advantage of his
absence to cast suspicion on his motives. And, besides, it
was important to keep the fires of indignation burning at
home if the delegation was to have any hope of success.

And success must have seemed very near. At about
the time the delegation was sailing for England, Lord
Durham was presenting to the British parliament his
now famous report on the state of the North American
colonies. This report delighted Howe, for after one short
summer in North America, Lord Durham had accurately
diagnosed the ills of the colonies. He prescribed responsible government as the only lasting remedy.

But there were men on both sides of the Atlantic who
did not share Howe's enthusiasm. The Legislative Council
in Halifax hastily passed resolutions condemning the

*Herbert Huntington, long-
time friend and political
colleague of Joseph Howe*

*What do you know about
Lord Durham and his
famous report?
On what grounds would its
recommendations have been
opposed?*

report. In England, the new Colonial Secretary, Lord John Russell, persuaded parliament that comparison of the colonial councils with the British cabinet was not valid. How could they govern if they were forced to resign every time a majority of the lower house voted against them? Such a policy could only result in separation of the colonies from Britain.

The Nova Scotia reformers were in despair, but Howe was not the man to give up without a fight. He wrote a series of four letters to Lord John Russell, ably pleading the case for responsible government. He pointed out that the granting of British constitutional privileges was less likely to result in separation than the denial of them. These letters Howe printed and sent to members of both British Houses and to the press. The delegation, meanwhile, returned in October 1839, having won many small victories but on the main constitutional issue totally defeated. When it presented its report, Howe moved resolutions of non-confidence in the Legislative Council.

Howe's letters had done their work, however, and even while the delegates were on their way home, Lord John Russell had sent dispatches to the governor-general stating that he had been commanded by Queen Victoria to administer the provinces "in accordance with the well-understood wishes and interests of the people and to pay to their feelings, as expressed through their representatives, the deference that is justly due to them."

The lieutenant-governor of New Brunswick, Sir John Harvey, took this to mean that the colonies had been granted responsible government and acted accordingly. But in Nova Scotia, the Council dug in its heels. In his reply to Howe's resolution of non-confidence, Sir Colin Campbell, now completely under the domination of the Council, said he did not believe the British government had changed its policy, and that he "had every reason to be satisfied with the advice and assistance which [the Council] have at all times afforded me."

Feeling ran so high at this insult that even James Uniacke, government leader in the lower house, resigned from the Council. He eventually became a close ally of Joseph Howe in the fight for reform. But the other members of Council clung to their positions of privilege, and a confrontation between the Assembly and the lieutenant-governor was now inevitable. An address to

Sir Colin Campbell himself having proved useless as expected, Howe moved an address to the Queen requesting the recall of the lieutenant-governor.

At a meeting in Halifax, both sides passionately aired their views. Here for the first time Howe found himself matched aginst J. W. Johnston, the Solicitor-General (who, incidentally, had represented John Howe many years before in the case of the lost apprentice). Johnston and Howe were to be bitter adversaries in many encounters to come. It was ironical that the governor's supporters, brought to their present position by their contempt for the will of the people, should now try to stir up popular support for their cause by distributing copies of Johnston's speech and by holding meetings all over the province.

In the midst of all this, Howe had an unpleasant adventure. Having publicly referred once again to the extravagant fees of the judges, he was challenged to a duel by the son of Chief Justice Halliburton (no relation to T. C. Haliburton). There had been such challenges in the past, and Howe knew there would be more unless he acted firmly. It was not an easy decision to make, however. His own courage never wavered, but he was deeply concerned for Susan Ann, in whose life there had already been enough tragedy. Since the trial she had borne three more children, two of whom had died when only a few months old. In a letter left to be given to Susan Ann if he should be killed in the duel, he said: "The future for you . . . might well unman me, and would, did I not feel that without a protector you could better face the world than with one whose courage was suspected, and who was liable to continual insult which he could not resent . . . There shall be no blood on my hand." In another letter left with his second (the loyal Herbert Huntington), to be published in the event of his death, Howe wrote: "I feel that I am bound to hazard my life rather than blight all prospects of being useful."

And so on a grey March morning, by the old martello tower in Point Pleasant Park, Joseph Howe and young John Halliburton faced each other. A fateful moment in Nova Scotia's history. Halliburton fired first, and missed. Howe, who was known to be an excellent shot, took careful aim. Halliburton waited. Then Howe, true to his word to Susan Ann, deliberately fired in the air. "Let the

J. W. Johnston, long-time political rival of Joseph Howe

The martello tower at Point Pleasant Park, Halifax, scene of Howe's duel with John Halliburton in 1840

creature live," he said, handing his pistol to Huntington. He had risked his life to make his point but, as he explained to his sister Jane, he had taught his opponents a lesson in "coolness and moderation," and had secured the "perfect independence . . . to explain or to apologize — to fight or refuse, in the future." He was justified only a few weeks later when on a similar pretext, Sir Rupert George, the provincial secretary, sent him another challenge. To this he replied that having no personal quarrel with Sir Rupert, "I should not fire at him if I went out, and that having no great fancy for being shot at, by every public officer whose intellect I might happen to compare with his emoluments, I begged leave to decline."

Meanwhile it was reported in Halifax that the Colonial Secretary had refused to present the address to the Queen. It appeared that Sir Colin Campbell would remain in office in defiance of the Assembly. This would have been an intolerable situation, and anger mounted in the province. But in July 1840, Governor-General Charles Thompson (later Lord Sydenham, for whom Howe's youngest son was named) arrived from Quebec and himself took control. In their accustomed manner, the Council members hastened to his side to begin their intrigues. They produced the letters to Lord John Russell as

evidence that Howe was a threat to law and order. But
Thompson was not so easily hoodwinked. He asked
Howe to explain and discuss the letters, which he did
to such effect that Sir Colin Campbell soon afterwards
returned to England. Not, however, without shaking
Howe's hand and receiving in his turn a tribute, in the
Novascotian, to his many virtues. When his successor,
Lord Falkland, arrived in September, Howe was invited to
join the Council.

*Lieutenant-Governor Sir
Colin Campbell, whose
removal from office was
brought about by Howe*

Chapter 7 Responsible Government: The Battle Won

Because of the jealousies and enmities that naturally arose from Howe's triumphant march of reform and political achievement, it is not surprising that many legends have sprung up about the wildness of his private life. Much has been said to blacken his character, but he would have been a rare man indeed had there been no weaknesses to set against his many and great strengths. He was a sociable man. In his younger days he was not averse to an occasional drinking party, and during his early travels he took a leading part in any gaiety that was going. The charge that he enjoyed "low" company must be considered in the light of the snobbery and malice of some of his political opponents. Unlike them, Howe did not consider himself superior to people who fished and farmed for a living. That he was a "ladies' man" is beyond doubt, and he was certainly not always faithful to Susan Ann. But there is no question, either, about the stability and contentment of his marriage and the deep mutual devotion between him and Susan Ann. His letters to her are largely concerned with business and affairs of state, but sometimes there surfaces a cry of profound homesickness and affection. Later, when celebrating his triumphs with friends far from home, his first thought was always "a toast to Mrs. Howe."

Susan Ann did not shirk her growing social obligations, but she was a "home body" at heart. It was as well, for although Howe tried hard to follow the example of his own father, and indeed won from his children much of the same love and respect, most of the responsibility for their upbringing must have fallen to Susan Ann. Although she had in all ten children, at least five of them died very young. But she was by no means the colourless character that all this domesticity may suggest. She was

a shrewd businesswoman, capable of managing the newspaper and the print shop while Howe was away. She is
credited with "taking a deep interest in her husband's
plans and sharing his victories and defeats during a
stormy political life," and with being "greatly esteemed
by her husband's associates." Her life was not made
easier by Howe's tendency to forget that he had invited
several people to dinner, or by his long unpredictable
hours of work.

In the middle years, at least, there was seldom enough
money. Howe has been portrayed as a place-seeker, but
for many years he declined all salaried posts, believing
that they would prejudice the "glorious independence" he
had fought for. It was only when he began to feel the
need for larger dragons to slay, and broader fields upon
which to slay them, that he began what has been unjustly
described as "one of the most humiliating and self-
debasing dunnings of Downing Street on record." He
firmly believed that the higher offices of empire should be
open to accomplished "colonials," and he was ambitious
enough, and sure enough of his own ability, to aspire to
such office. But he let pass many opportunities that were
in conflict with his high ideals of honesty and duty.
Finally, he has been described with some truth as
arrogant and egotistical. It is not difficult, however, to
distinguish between the swagger of Howe the electioneer,
the inspired eloquence of Howe the legislator, and the
occasional self-doubt of Howe the private man.

Joe Howe was re-elected in November 1840 with
a large majority, and when the House met in February
he was elected Speaker. His troubles were not over,
however. Although the reformers now had four representatives on the Council, and it had been agreed that any
member of Council who lost popular support should
resign, Howe had won these reforms by consenting
to a coalition, an arrangement for sharing the responsi-
bilities of government with his opponents. Herbert
Huntington, convinced that this could not work, would
neither join nor support the coalition. Several other
reformers, seeing the coalition as a betrayal, took the
same line.

Huntington proved to be right. Several eminent Tory
members, including J. W. Johnston, made speeches
denying, in effect, that there had been any constitutional

*What is the significance of
Downing Street?*

*The Speaker's chair in
Province House, the Nova
Scotia House of Assembly,
occupied by Howe from
1840-43*

change. Throughout the coalition's two years of shaky
existence, they paid only lip service to their responsibility to the Assembly, while their supporters in the
public employ did all they could to make it appear that
the reforms were not working. Lord Falkland's liberalism
soon began to waver. The new Tory government in
Britain had instructed him to oppose party government
in Nova Scotia and party government, if the coalition
failed, was sure to come.

The government planned to stop supporting colleges
run by religious bodies, and it was at the height of this
battle, while Howe was absent, that Lord Falkland was
persuaded by Johnston to dissolve the House. After the
resulting election, which was indecisive, the lieutenant-
governor appointed a Council unfairly weighted in
favour of the Tories. Howe and his reform colleagues
resigned their Council seats in protest.

For the next four years, from the opposition side of
the House, Howe carried on a running battle against Lord
Falkland, and devoted most of his energy to expanding
and strengthening the reform party. Falkland, for his

Thomas Chandler Haliburton

part, conducted the fight with increasing, unstatesman-
like malice. Howe had earlier sold the *Novascotian*,
but now, to further the cause of reform and to defend
himself against the growing Tory smear campaign in the
Morning Post, he took the editor's chair again. Under
extreme provocation he published several lampoons, in
rather poor taste, against the lieutenant-governor. This
exchange of insults did neither side credit, and Howe's
part in it may well have damaged his reputation and
prospects.

Howe's frustration at this period was deepened by a
quarrel of growing bitterness with his old friend T. C.
Haliburton. In 1838, the two men had made the "grand
tour" of Europe together, during which they formed a
deep attachment. They travelled extensively in the
British Isles, France, Belgium and Germany. Throughout
the tour, but especially in London and Paris, they got
through an incredible amount of sightseeing. In London,
they visited the Tower, the Zoo, Kew Gardens, Hampton
Court maze, Smithfield Market, the Houses of Parliament, Westminster Abbey and a score of other places
still familiar to the tourist of today. They caught glimpses
of Queen Victoria at Ascot races and at Windsor Castle.

Among the many plays they saw were two starring the world-renowned actor William Macready, by whom Howe was not greatly impressed. In Paris, they went to the Louvre, the Tuilleries palace and gardens, Notre Dame Cathedral, the Champs Elysées, and so on.

Towards the end of the tour, Howe was getting "savage and anxious" because he had received no mail, and Susan Ann was expecting another child (a son, James, who was to die within the year). He was also suffering acute discomfort, as he journeyed north into Scotland, because he had foolishly brought only one pair of very thin boots. In spite of these annoyances, however, the tour was a great success and amid its many adventures the friendship between Howe and Haliburton flourished.

But as the political struggle intensified in the months to come, a rift appeared in the relationship. Haliburton in some of his writings of this period made indirect but unmistakably insulting references to Howe. The friendship turned rapidly into open enmity. It would take many years, and all the resources of Howe's generous spirit, to heal the breach.

"Clifton," the home of Thomas Chandler Haliburton at Windsor, Nova Scotia, completed in 1836. It is now owned by the Nova Scotia Museum and is open to the public

Plaque in the House of Assembly, Halifax, commemorating the winning of responsible government

Who were the Whigs? What was their most important contribution to the growth of the British political system?

Howe's anguish during these four dark years was further increased by a growing burden of debt. People who owed him money would not pay. And Haliburton's failure to keep certain promises that would have given Howe a substantial income from the successful "Clockmaker" series rendered the situation desperate.

By the fall of 1844, however, he was able to write to Jane that "the smoke was clearing away and . . . I could see daylight all around me," and that "The first appeal to the People will set all to rights." That appeal was not to come for two years, by which time the Whigs had returned to power in England and the sympathetic Lord John Russell had become prime minister. In Nova Scotia, Lord Falkland had been replaced by Sir John Harvey, a tactful man who favoured reform.

The time at last was ripe. In the election of 1847, Howe's reformers were victorious. Returning to his farm at Musquodoboit in August, triumphant but exhausted after a hard campaign, Howe was met 22 kilometres from home by a jubilant crowd and escorted back by a mounted procession more than 500 metres long. When the festivities were over, Joe Howe, back among the plain folk he loved, took one of the rare holidays of his life. "For a month I did nothing but play with the children, and read old books to my girls. I then went into the woods and called moose with the old hunters, camping night after night, listening to their stories, calming my thoughts with the perfect stillness of the forest and forgetting the bitterness of conflict amidst the beauties of nature."

When the new House met in January 1848, J. W. Johnston and his followers were forced to resign on a vote of non-confidence, and the first fully responsible government in any British colony took office in Halifax, with James Uniacke as leader and Joseph Howe as provincial secretary.

The Railway Chapter 8

Even in the days of his "rambles," Joe Howe had re-
marked how Nova Scotia's mining industry might be
made more profitable by the use of railways. By 1835,
he was publicly advocating construction of a line linking
Halifax and Windsor, on which "a single engine will
travel, with a weight of ninety tons in its train . . . at
eight miles an hour; and, managed by three men and
thirteen boys, will bring, in five and a half hours, to
market, as much . . . produce as could be brought on the
common road by two hundred and seventy horses and
ninety men in a long summer day."

Now that the fight for responsible government was
won, Howe's enormous mental and physical energy
needed new challenges. He was to find them in his railway dream. Nova Scotia's human and material resources,
he insisted, must be used to the best advantage of her

Halifax about 1853

people; and, of course, to the glory of the empire, since for Howe this was the framework into which everything must fit. In 1849, while helping to reshape the government in accordance with its new responsibility to the people, Howe was also working for a broadened and improved system of education, disputing with the leaders of an increasingly ugly rebellion in the Canadas, and finding time to write patriotic poems to mark the centenary of Halifax. But railways were fast becoming the focus of his interest.

From the first, Howe maintained that railways should be financed and controlled by government. This, of course, put him in direct conflict with men of influence who hoped to make their fortunes out of the railways. In March 1850, Howe called on the provincial government to finance the whole of the Halifax-Windsor project. The government refused to cover more than half the cost, and Howe was forced to agree, having been assured by the opponents of his scheme that the rest of the money could be easily raised by a private company. They were mistaken. Construction of the line was delayed four years, and then had to be undertaken on Howe's original terms.

Such difficulty with a comparatively minor project did not promise well for two much larger undertakings that were being widely discussed. The first of these, a line from Halifax to Quebec, had been recommended by Lord Durham a decade earlier. Extensive surveys had been carried out, and the provinces involved had pledged large sums in the belief that the British government would guarantee the remainder. Work seemed as good as started. Then, less than four months after Howe's disappointment over the Windsor line, word came from London that no support from that quarter was to be hoped for.

In the light of this setback, it is surprising with what enthusiasm a party of men set out, within days, for Portland, Maine, to discuss plans for a railway linking that city with Halifax. Among the group were James Uniacke and Howe's old adversary J. W. Johnston. They were received with great warmth and hospitality, and much was made of the fact that this was the first such cooperative enterprise since the American Revolution. The meeting indeed seems to have generated more

emotion than clear thinking, but the delegates came
back full of determination.

They held a meeting in Halifax to present their report.
They admitted they had no idea how the $12 million
needed for the scheme was to be raised, yet they managed
to persuade the meeting to pass a resolution approving
the line as proposed. They were appointing a committee
to carry the matter further when Howe, unable to remain
aloof any longer, mounted the platform. On the spur of
the moment, he made a long impassioned speech, with all
the facts and figures at his command, easily convincing
the meeting that private capital was not to be counted
upon. His resolution calling on the Nova Scotia government to undertake construction of that part of the line
within its borders was unanimously passed and warmly
applauded. "Men who had not spoken to Mr. Howe for
years," wrote his friend William Annand, "were loudest
in the expression of their approbation."

Less than a week after the meeting, Lieutenant-
Governor Sir John Harvey's letter supporting the plan
and seeking a British guarantee for any needed loans was
on its way to London. But the reply from Colonial
Secretary Lord Grey was not encouraging. Rather than
abandon its scheme, however, the provincial government
sent Howe to England in November 1850. He was to try
to win over Lord Grey on the question of a guarantee; or,
failing that, to explore the possibilities of raising the
money without it.

*A "piggyback" ticket. What
was the "piggyback"?*

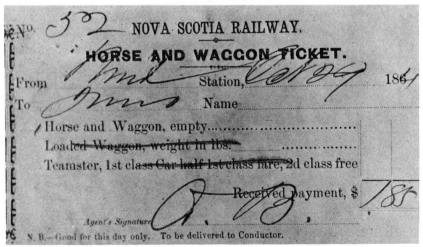

Howe left on November 1, 1850, equipped with a list of important people he wanted to meet, several pages of notes for stories to be told on various occasions, and a list of things to buy for himself and the ladies of his family. For Howe it was to be a memorable visit, although he began it with some misgivings. Arrogant and egotistical he may sometimes have been, but he had his moments of humility and self-doubt. Here was a Bluenose lad, unsophisticated and unschooled, come to pit his powers of persuasion against the most influential members of the British nobility. Arrived in London "with its two millions of people around me, of whom I knew not ten," how impertinent must have seemed his dream of rallying the British public behind his cause. But at such times of supreme test he could usually count on what he called "one of my flashes." And on this ocassion it did not let him down. "Knowledge," he wrote "which I never acquired by study, flashed into my mind as if by inspiration."

He suddenly saw his visit not as a mere fund-raising mission. He had a vision of the glorious future of the empire in which the North American colonies would play a significant role as partners, and in which the railways would become the vital arteries of colonization and commerce. He dreamed of a system of government in which colonial representatives would sit in the British parliament to champion their far-off peoples. He convincingly argued that the railways would benefit Great Britain as much as they did her colonies. Not only would they stimulate trade and development; not only would they assist the expansion of the empire and make it easier to defend: they would provide a means of emptying the overcrowded prisons and poorhouses that burdened the British taxpayer. Under Howe's scheme, the prisoners and the poor would work on the railways, and be given land grants and financial assistance to settle near the line as it broke new ground.

In arguing all this, Howe did not rely on inspiration alone. He read "a cartload of books and pamphlets." He made frequent and telling use of the statistics gleaned from these, disproving for the hundredth time the jibe of a political opponent that the only figures he knew were figures of speech. Lord Grey, at any rate, was impressed. He had read Howe's proposal, he said, with the attention its great importance deserved. Which, Joe Howe wrote in his journal, was "pretty well from a Minister of State to a poor bluenose far away from his friends."

Between periods of intense activity in furthering his plan there were long intervals of anxious waiting. But Howe was not one to waste time. He went systematically down his visiting list, with so much success that he was able to report having dined with "Dickens, Littleton, Landseer, Macready, Forster, White, and had gin punch and lark pudding." He also went to see Carlyle and Thackeray. He attended the Lord Mayor of London's banquet and ball, and the famous Chelsea Ball at Christmas. He went to the theatre many times, including a performance by Macready as Brutus, when he found the great actor "terribly shaky and hoarse."

But the social highlight of Howe's visit was his presentation to the Queen at St. James's Palace, by Lord Grey. As the time for this approached, Howe grew extremely nervous, "having to learn to go down on one knee gracefully, keeping my hat and sword out of my own and everybody else's way. . . . I would rather face the House of Commons a thousand times. I would compromise, kissing the Maids of Honour all round, having the Duchess of Sutherland thrown in." And when the great moment came: "I look at nothing else but Her Majesty and think of nothing else but measuring the distance and executing the manoeuvre properly . . . . Tall fellow beside her — suppose it is Prince Albert — but dare not look . . . and here goes Bluenose — a look —a step — and my knee is bent before my sovereign and her little hand at my lips . . . there is no time for sentiment or emotion." Then before he could recover, "Earl Grey springs at me, seizes my hand and, in a moment, I am shaking hands with Johnny Russell and chatting with the great head of the Whigs and late Premier of England."

In his official business there were many ups and downs. Two weeks after Lord Grey's favourable comments on Howe's letter outlining his scheme, he sent Howe an official refusal of his request for guarantees. Howe, suffering from a lung infection and "not in good trim to fight an Imperial Government and agitate England," resolved, however, to do just that. He returned to the attack. At the beginning of a two-hour interview with Lord Grey and his under-secretary Benjamin

Hawes, Howe found them "both looking grim and self-complacent." But by the end of it, the letter of refusal had been withdrawn, and Howe had won permission to plead his case further and to sound out British public opinion. This he did in a forcible public address at Southampton on 14 January, 1851. In this, the railways received little direct mention, but the need for credit guarantees was skilfully interwoven, as Howe elaborated his ideas for a broad imperial policy aimed at the settlement and development of the colonies for the common benefit. This speech won the attention of both Houses of Parliament and was widely and favourably commented upon in the press. Howe's reputation was greatly increased on both sides of the Atlantic, especially when he was able to report back to Halifax that Lord Grey "would ask Parliament to advance or guarantee the funds which may be required" for both the Quebec and Portland lines. Howe celebrated by drinking the health of Mrs. Howe and Earl Grey.

At home, an election was in the offing. Howe, returning in triumph from his mission ("home, thank God"), threw himself into the task of strengthening popular support for his railway project. There were still doubters, even in his own party. A complicating factor had been introduced into the debate by the arrival of a Mr. Charles Archibald representing a group Howe had met in England, who claimed that if given the contract for building the proposed railways, they could as "co-partners" effect considerable savings. J. W. Johnston and many others in all the provinces concerned were attracted by Archibald's proposals, but Howe indignantly opposed them. For six years, he said, no one had offered to risk money in the venture. Mr. Archibald's friends had not come forward when he arrived in England in search of capital. But now when it appeared that seven million pounds could be raised without risk to them, they were anxious to become co-partners in the spending of it. Howe's sincerity and logic carried the day. The election was won, though narrowly, and in September 1851, Howe's Railway Bills were passed by a comfortable majority.

The ink was hardly dry on them when Lord Grey wrote to say that he had intended his guarantees to apply only to the Quebec and not to the Portland line. This effectively scuttled Howe's grand design, for various reasons. One was that if there was to be only one line, New Brunswick insisted that it should follow the already settled St. John River Valley, instead of opening up new territory for the colonization upon which Howe's whole plan was based. Howe took full responsibility for the "misundertsanding" with Lord Grey, but it is highly probable that underhand pressures had been brought to bear on the Colonial Secretary.

Still determined that Nova Scotia should control its share of the modified project, Howe obtained promises of financing and introduced bills for that purpose. But Mr.

NOVA SCOTIA RAILWAY.

TARIFF.

PASSENGERS.

Morning and Evening Trains run daily between Halifax and Grand Lake, and a Mid-day Train to and from Bedford.

Miles.	Stations.	1st Train.	2d Train.	3d Train.	Fares. 1st Class.	Fares. 2d Class.
	Up Trains.	A. M.	Noon.	P. M.	s. d.	s. d.
	Halifax, depart	7.30	12. 0	3. 0		
3¼	Four Mile House	7.40	12 10	3.10	0 7½	0 5
8	Bedford	8. 0	12 30	3.30	1 3	0 10
10¾	Scott Road	8.10		3.40	1 10	1 3
13¼	Windsor Junction				2 3	1 6
20	Fletcher's	8 40		4.10	3 4	2 3
22½	Grand Lake, arrive	8.50		4.20	3 9	2 6
	Down Trains.	A. M.	P. M.	P. M.	s. d.	s. d.
	Grand Lake, depart	9.25		5.10		
2½	Fletcher's	9.35		5.20	0 5	0 4
9¼	Windsor Junction				1 6	1 0
11¾	Scott Road	10.15		5.50	1 11	1 3
14½	Bedford	10.25	1.45	6.	2 6	1 9
19¼	Four Mile House	10.45	2. 5	6.20	3 2	2 8
22½	Halifax, arrive	10.55	2.15	6.30	3 9	2 6

Excursion Tickets—for use same day, up and down—a rate and a half. Tickets for Children under 12 years of age, half price. Passengers not providing themselves with tickets before entering the Cars, will be required to pay 7½d. extra. Special Trains provided on reasonable notice, and Passenger Cars hired to parties or families at diminished rates.

HORSES & CARRIAGES.

	Bedford. s. d.	Grand Lake s. d.
1 Horse and empty Carriage	1 10½	2 9
1 do. Carriage and load	2 6	3 9
Driver in Horse Car	0 7½	1 0
2 Horses and empty Carriage	3 1½	4 8
2 do. Carriage and load	3 9	5 6
Driver in Horse Car	0 7½	1 0
3 Horses and empty Carriage	4 4½	6 8
3 do. Carriage and load	5 [illegible]	[illegible] 6
Driver in Horse Car	0 7½	1 0
4 Horses and empty Carriage	5 0	7 6
4 do. Carriage and load	6 3	9 6
Driver in Horse Car	0 7½	1 0
Saddle or other Horse	1 6	2 3

MISCELLANEOUS.

Small Parcels and Packages according to size and value.	Bedford. s. d.	Grand Lake s. d.
Barrels, each	0 4	0 7½
Hhds. and Puns., 80 to 120 galls.	1 3	2 0
Bags of 2 bushels	0 3	0 5
Do. of 3 do.	0 4	0 7½
Bundles, equal in size to a barrel	0 4	0 7½
Heavy Articles, by weight, per ton, per mile	0 3	
Furniture, per ten cubic feet, at	0 5	0 7½
Dry Fish, in bundles of 1 cwt	0 2	0 4
Parcels under 50 lbs. or bulk of half-barrel size	0 3	0 4
Cordwood, per cord	2 6	3 9
Bark	2 6	3 9
Lumber and Scantling, per M.	2 0	3 0
Screwed Hay, per ton	2 6	3 9
Shingles, per 4 bundles	1 0	1 6
Timber, per ton, per mile	0 3	
Do. per M. soft	2 9	4 0
Do. per M. hard	3 3	5 0
Calves and Pigs, each	0 4	0 6
Sheep	0 3	0 4
Neat Cattle, single	0 10	1 3
Do. when more than one	0 8	1 0

The rates between Bedford and Grand Lake are the same as those between Halifax and Bedford. Freight taken in quantity by agreement. Freight to be labelled or marked legibly in all cases—unless so marked, transportation will be at freighter's risk. No responsibility assumed by carriers, unless contents of packages or parcels are distinctly and legibly marked upon them ☞ No Horses, Carriages, or other freight received within ten minutes before the starting of Trains In all cases the Cars to be loaded and discharged at expense of freighters—and not loaded above the stancheons.

JOSEPH HOWE, Chairman.

N. S. Railway Office, Feb. 2, 1857.

Nova Scotia Railway timetable, 1857

Archibald and his friends had already made deals with Canada and New Brunswick, and Howe was forced, very much against his will, to do the same. He insisted, however, that if the work had not been started in six months the government would take control. Since at the end of that time not a spike had been driven, nor a tree felled, Howe at last got his way.

On 4 April, 1854, Joseph Howe gave up the office of provincial secretary and was appointed Chief Commissioner of the Railway Board. Ten months later, the first section of the line was open for traffic. Howe's wisdom in fighting for government control was amply demonstrated in the next few years. While all manner of difficulties and scandals beset the other provinces, the railway work in Nova Scotia went smoothly ahead and the record of the Railway Board was without blemish.

Gourley's Shanty Chapter 9

During 1854, while much of his thought and energy were
being devoted to the realization of his railroad dream,
things were happening half a world away that would
have strange consequences for Joe Howe. Britain and
France were engaged in an inept and muddled war with
Russia in the Crimea. Throughout the winter, the armies
confronting each other at Sebastopol were so ravaged by
disease and bitter weather that only half the British
troops were fit for service.

Where is the Crimea? How did Britain become involved in a war there?

As early as 1846, and again in February 1854, Howe
had made proposals concerning the "Organization of the
Empire," which had included military support of the
mother country by the colonies in this sort of emergency.
These suggestions having fallen on deaf ears, the British
government by the middle of that black winter passed a
bill approving the enlistment of troops from foreign
countries. In the United States, economic conditions had
produced much hardship, and it was reported that willing recruits would be plentiful.

Accordingly, in March 1855, Howe and a secretary
went to the United States. Their mission was to channel
prospective recruits to Halifax for enlistment. The
suggestion had been Howe's but he went with the full
approval of the lieutenant-governor and with the knowledge and collaboration of John Crampton, the British
Ambassador in Washington. Since the United States was
neutral, the operation was ethically and legally dubious,
but Howe's anguish at the British plight in the Crimea
was so real that he would have broken any law in the
book. "There is no prison so loathesome in which I would
not cheerfully have spent five years, to have placed five
regiments, in the spring of 1855, under the walls of
Sebastopol."

All would probably have been well had it not been for
a small but militant group of Irish Catholics in Halifax.
The violent anti-British sentiments of this group did not
reflect the opinion of the province's Catholics as a whole,
but its activities were bound to inflame passions in moder-
ate people and awaken old hatreds. An organ of the

Why would the Irish Catholics in Halifax be pleased by the British reverses in the war?

Irish faction, the *Halifax Catholic*, consistently baited the Protestants and hailed with delight the British misfortunes in the Crimea. This infuriated the patriotic Howe. He was further provoked when William Condon, one of the leaders of the group, met a batch of Irish recruits from the United States and persuaded them not to enlist. Condon then informed the New York press that 60 Irishmen had been lured to Nova Scotia as railway labourers, with the object of enlistment for service in the Crimea.

The unwelcome publicity put an end to Howe's usefulness in the United States. Had he stayed, he would doubtless have been arrested, and might not have been so fortunate as his secretary, who was, in fact, brought to trial and acquitted. For in the opinion of the United States Attorney-General, Howe's activities were "a hostile attack" on United States sovereignty. Ambassador Crampton was recalled to London. The matter was debated in the British parliament, and Crampton was sharply attacked by future Prime Minister W. E. Gladstone. In response to Gladstone's speech, Howe wrote and published a long, strongly worded rebuttal.

But it was the consequences at home that most profoundly affected Howe. Angry as he was at the racial and religious mud-slinging of the *Halifax Catholic* and the treachery of Condon, he never once in all this time took up his pen in protest. The provocation had its effect, however, on Howe's Protestant railway workers, who returned measure for measure by ridiculing certain religious beliefs of their Catholic workmates. Anger mounted too high for words. One night the Catholic workers attacked the shanty (hut) of a man named Gourley and savagely beat up a group of Protestants assembled there. Howe, determined not to let "a handful of Irishmen . . . drive all other classes off our public works," brought the offenders to trial. When, six months later, they were acquitted on a split jury vote and the *Halifax Catholic*, interpreting this as a rebuke for the Protestants, resumed its old taunts, Howe's fury broke bounds. In a letter to the *Morning Chronicle* he wrote: "The right to discuss all questions and doctrines . . . and to laugh at what we believe to be absurd, is the common right of every Nova Scotian; and all the 'mercurial people' [the Irish] that can be mustered will never

Melville Island, Halifax (the subject of Howe's early poem), with the barracks where troops recruited by him in the United States for service in the Crimea were quartered

trample it out of our hearts. . . ." Later in the letter a note
of threat crept in:

"Mércurial Irishmen will do well to remember that . . . they are
but a handful of the population. . . . Their best security is law and
order, and the preservation of the free institutions of the country.
There is no part of Nova Scotia where they could not be trampled
down in a day, were the people to become 'mercurial,' and deal
out the 'brotherly love and forebearance' which were displayed
at Gourlay's Shantie . . . ."

Howe pointed out that in no Catholic country would
a dissenting paper have the freedom enjoyed by the
Halifax Catholic, yet the more extreme Catholics sought
to deny the Protestants that same freedom. He asserted
the right of any man to laugh at another's beliefs. "I
respect the feelings and admire the sincerity of the
Catholic whose opinions I do not share. . . . But when he
comes to propagate his religion by the bludgeon —
when the liberty to critize and scoff, which he claims and
exercises, he attempts to deny to the Protestant population, my path is plain, and I tread it utterly regardless of
consequences."

The consequences were painful. A secession of the
Catholics from Howe's party left it so weakened that at
the opening of the new session in February 1857, J. W.
Johnston moved a vote of non-confidence in the government. Howe felt morally bound to relinquish his position
on the Railway Board. Several years later, when the
Liberals returned to power, the Catholics refused to take
cabinet seats under Howe. As a result of all this, politics
in Nova Scotia were poisoned by religious rancour for
many years to come.

Howe himself seems to have been concerned less with
matters of doctrine than with the principle of tolerance.
Although his faith was profound, it did not fit into any
narrowly defined sect. His father was a Sandemanian.
Howe inherited much of his piety, but already by very
early manhood, while the family was at church, he
preferred to let his worship manifest itself in silent enjoy-
ment of wild nature.

Thus was the man whose first act on entering the
Assembly had been an appeal for religious tolerance,
and who ever since had worked to tear down the barriers
of bigotry, forced by circumstances into a religious feud
of enduring bitterness.

Chapter 10 **A Vision of Unity**

Although responsible government had been established in Nova Scotia for more than a decade, it was still possible for the Johnston administration to cling to office from May 1859 to February 1860 after the people's mandate had been withdrawn. This they did, with the backing of Lieutenant-Governor Lord Mulgrave, on the shallow pretext that several Liberal members were disqualified by holding paid public office. Lord Mulgrave, petitioned by more than half the members to call the House together, "declined to accept advice from other than his constitutional advisers."

When at last the House was convened, the government was defeated by a narrow vote and the Liberals took office. Seven months later Premier William Young was made Chief Justice of the Supreme Court and Joseph Howe became leader of the government.

It is ironical that from this distance of time political events during Howe's term of office as premier do not emerge as "historic." There were none of those great challenges to which he had risen so splendidly in earlier years, and to which he would rise again with perhaps less glory but with undiminished fire in the years to come. Yet he was working harder than ever, at one point to the peril of his health. "I never went through a more laborious session," he recorded in his diary. "I rarely left the House in the lunchhour but kept up my correspondence from 1 to 3, then often sat to 8 or 9 with no food but a few figs and crackers and a glass of water."

What, then, was achieved by all this labour? Howe engaged in one more long abortive struggle to reconcile all the conflicting forces that impeded his cherished inter-colonial railway scheme, making two further visits to England for this purpose. Returning from the second of these he felt as joyfully triumphant as on that earlier occasion more than a decade before. In an ecstatic letter to Jane, who after all those years was still his pen pal and confidante, he said that the trip was "for many reasons one of the most gratifying and triumphant I have ever had." There was "only one last detail" not yet settled to

Joseph Howe about the time he was premier of Nova Scotia

his entire satisfaction. But history was sadly to repeat
itself. There were too many political sores in the colonies
even for Howe's diplomacy to heal, and all his work once
more was brought to nothing. But the trip was not wasted.
In the same letter he confided to his sister: "... my old
friend Lord Russell has bestowed upon me, in the most
gracious manner, the Commissionership of Fisheries. ...
The salary and allowances are very much better than I
get as Secretary, and besides, I can live where I like."
He goes on with an excusable hint of snobbery: "I spent
a couple of delightful days with the Duke of New-
castle. ..."

The chief provincial issue during all this period concerned the right to vote. For some years all adult males
in the province had been eligible. But there were poor
and unscrupulous minorities whose votes could be purchased, and in some key constituencies these votes could
be manipulated to affect the outcome. Since most of the
wealth was in the hands of Howe's opponents, the
Liberals claimed they suffered by this abuse. And so by
another of Fate's little jokes, Joe Howe, the champion of
government by the people, found himself the chief ad-
vocate of a bill to disfranchise all who did not own
property in the province. But Fate added an additional
twist. The upper house decreed that the bill should not
take effect until after the next election, with the predict-
able result that those who would have lost the franchise
voted against the government. The Liberals were defeated and Howe lost his seat in the Assembly. The ring-
ing tones of his oratory would not be heard there again.
It did not apparently strike him as odd that his last
speech — he who had won responsible government and
so armed the people against the power of wealth —
should be a contradiction of the principle he held must
dear.

Perhaps the most significant thing about Howe's
years as premier was the emergence of a new antagonist
— Dr. Charles Tupper. In Howe's one great remaining
battle, even his traditional opponent J. W. Johnston was
to be overshadowed by this newcomer. Throughout that
period Tupper lost no opportunity to harass the government and to provoke Howe personally. He sought to
make party capital out of everything, to Howe's great
exasperation.

Why would the office of Commissioner of Fisheries be considered so important and be so well paid?

Dr. Charles Tupper about the time of his early differ-ences with Howe

What do you know about the subsequent career of Dr. Charles Tupper?

"Did he name a day — give notice of his intention — and get up a good rattling party attack, once a fortnight, or once a month, it would be all right; but these little, perpetual, peddling, snarling assaults, on all subjects, on all occasions, make himself and his party objects of pity, and do not in any wise advance their interests."

Tupper revived the old controversy about Howe's recruiting activities in the United States, claiming that Howe's past conflict with the American authorities would impair his ability to do his job as Fisheries Commissioner. This was a blow below the belt, and it embittered Howe yet more against the man who, within a few years, was to lead (or, as many saw it, to force) Nova Scotia into Confederation. Although ~~Turner~~ *Tuppe* went on to become a Father of Confederation, a baronet and, briefly, prime minister of Canada, he was in many ways a lesser man

The House of Assembly library

than Joe Howe. He happened to be on the right side at the right time.

During 1864, the year following his defeat, with Tupper now in the premier's chair, Howe made two significant speeches. One was long, one short; one well considered, the other ill; one non-political, the other, so far as Howe was concerned, political dynamite. The first, delivered before the St. George's Society to mark the three hundredth anniversary of the birth of Shakespeare, gives us a glimpse of one of Howe's dream-selves: the scholar, the man of letters, the Samuel Johnson of Nova Scotia — the man he might have become, had he been true to poetry, the maiden he loved, instead of pursuing the harridan, politics. Several times during his career this dream-self briefly and wistfully surfaces, and we watch him indulging fantasies in which he turns his back on the vexatious world of politics to retire among his books in some idyllic retreat.

But the harridan now drags, now wheedles him back into the arena. He loves Nova Scotia too much, and reveres the British connection too deeply, to sit idly by while misguided men do harm to the one or violence to the other. And it is this love and this reverence that first cloud and later clear his judgment. So that on a warm night in August 1864, at a banquet honouring dignitaries from the other colonies, warmed a little perhaps by the wine and seduced by the vision of unity and peace among men, he makes a speech that will come back to haunt him. "I am not one of those." he says, "who thank God that I am a Nova Scotian merely, for I am a Canadian as well. I have never thought I was a Nova Scotian, but I look across the broad continent at the great territory which the Almighty has given us for an inheritance, and studied the mode by which it could be consolidated, the mode by which it could be united. . . . And why should union not be brought about? . . . I am pleased to think the day is rapidly approaching when the Provinces will be united, with one flag above our heads, one thought in all our bosoms, one Sovereign and one constitution."

Who was Dr. Samuel Johnson?
For what was he chiefly known?
Why would he be admired by Joseph Howe?

Province House, Halifax, the scene of Howe's political battles from 1836 to 1864.

Chapter 11 **A Torment of Indecision**

What name is now given to the men who gathered at Charlottetown for this conference? See how many of them you can name.

Only three days after that imprudent speech, Fisheries Commissioner Howe, already embarked in a British warship for a duty mission to Newfoundland, received a brief note signed "C. Tupper." It asked if Howe would go as a delegate to a conference at Charlottetown, where the union of the Maritime Provinces was to be discussed. Was Tupper persuaded by Howe's after-dinner remarks that here at last was a cause great enough to transcend their mutual hostility, or was this the first strand of a cunning web in which Tupper hoped Joe Howe would at last ensnare himself? Howe, at any rate, felt compelled by the pressure of his duties to decline; but, he added, "I . . . will be very happy to co-operate in carrying out any measure upon which the conference shall agree."

What the conference agreed upon, however, Joe Howe was neither happy nor willing to help carry out. For representatives of the lately — and precariously — united Canadas had persuaded the conference that its aims should be broadened to include union of all the provinces, and the meeting was to reconvene at Quebec City in October to discuss this proposal. Howe privately professed himself "glad to be out of the mess," but on the issue itself he reserved judgment. He attended several meetings called in Halifax to discuss it, but did not declare himself. He thought much, however. He had long favoured Maritime union but although, as his recent words indicated, he dreamed of an ultimate joining together of all the provinces in nationhood, he had often in the past warned of the perils of hasty union.

By January 1865, these perils far outweighed in his mind the advantages of early confederation, and he could keep silent no longer. On 11 January appeared the first of twelve articles on "The Botheration Scheme." In any system of representation based on population, Howe saw Nova Scotia losing all control of her destiny, becoming embroiled in the internal — and perhaps

external — strife of the Canadas, and getting little or
nothing in return. As early as 1838, he had written in
the *Novascotian* that "Nova Scotia was one of the
smallest of the Colonies, and might suffer in the arrangement." And in place of the current difficulties in
dealing with the far-off Colonial Office, he foresaw Nova
Scotia being governed by "an office in the back woods of
Canada, more difficult of access than that in London." He
several times asserted that completion of the intercolonial
railway must precede any step towards political union.
In view of the slowness of travel in those days, especially
in winter when the St. Lawrence was closed, his anxieties
were real.

In Howe's mind, union of all the colonies would
mean virtual independence from Britain, and since there
were in Canada strong voices in favour of annexation to
the United States, he was very wary of submitting Nova
Scotia to Canadian domination. He was not sure that the
Upper Provinces were capable of governing themselves,
let alone the Maritimes.

*Why would cooperation
between the United States
and the Maritime Provinces
be regarded as so significant
at this point in history?*

"Here" [he wrote] "we have peace and order, everybody worships
God as he pleases, and everybody obeys the law. There are no
armed midnight processions — no villains chalking our doors at
night — no arms secreted — no Fenians drilling — and everybody
sleeps in his bed securely, with no man to make him afraid. In
the name of common sense, then, are we to peril these blessings,
and mix ourselves up with distractions, the end of which no living
man can foresee?"

*Who were the Fenians?
What were their aims, and
how did they attempt to
achieve them?*

He was appalled, too, at the apparent haste with which
the change was to be brought about. In contrast to the
British constitution, developed over centuries, and the
American, over which great minds deliberated for
months, "The Quebec Constitution was framed in a
fortnight, amidst exhausting festivities. " What Howe
advocated was the working out of common economic
and defence policies, facilitated by improved communications, and letting political ties grow as the needs and the
benefits became evident.

While the Confederation storm was brewing, Joe
Howe was faced with anxieties of his own. His appointment as Fisheries Commissioner was almost over and the
British government did not seem about to offer him another. He was now 62. He had abandoned his newspaper
and printing business in favour of a career in politics,
which brought no pay. He had raised a large family. The

paid offices he had held had not enabled him to stave off debt. This was his situation early in 1866 when he was offered the editorship of the New York *Albion* for the dazzling salary of $3,500 a year. There was an alternate proposal for him to contribute articles to the paper for $1,500 a year, which would not require him to live in New York. Elated, he wrote to Susan Ann, "If they [the British Government] give me anything I can make up $1,500 by light labour and get my salary besides. If they give me nothing we can live here in our usual quiet way and put by $1,000 to pay our debts each year. . . . For this un-expected mercy I fervently thank God."

But by now it was becoming evident that Tupper had every intention of taking Nova Scotia into Confederation without seeking a mandate from the people: the people for whom Joe Howe had fought so long and so hard to obtain the right to make their voice heard in just such a crisis as this. Howe's dream of a quiet, financially secure future was swept away in a torment of indecision. Surely, after all the "thankless care and labour," such peace and security was owing to Susan Ann in her declining years, if not to Howe himself. Here at last was a chance to give it to her. And yet there was "poor old Nova Scotia, God help her, beset with marauders outside and enemies within, she has a hard time of it, and my mouth closed and my pen silent." For the first time in his life, he said, he hesitated between duty and interest. Not for long, however.

Why was Howe unable to speak out at this time? To whom was he referring as "marauders" outside and enemies within"?

By April 1866, Joe Howe was back, ready for battle. Pausing only long enough to get off several public and private letters outlining his stand, he set forth on a tour of the western counties, making speeches, rallying the people, meeting old friends; and, like a veteran recalled to active service, no doubt enjoying every minute of it. A couple of weeks earlier he had complained of being "lonely, weary, vexed." Now, he spoke with so much fight, that to the old-timers it must have seemed as though the young, irrepressible Joe Howe of 1828 was back again on his rambles, decrying their follies, proclaiming their rights, urging them to their duty. He reported on his return that he "could not find five hundred confederates on the whole tour."

In July 1866, Howe led a delegation to England to lobby against the proposed act of union. They set about

it with a will, obtaining audience with any person of influence who might plead their case, writing letters, seeking to awaken public interest in their cause. Howe also
published a long pamphlet, "Confederation Considered
in Relation to the Interests of the Empire." Some of his
arguments today may seem extravagant and even a little
hysterical, and it is all too easy in retrospect to ridicule,
as some biographers have done, his opposition to confederation. Such ridicule betrays complete lack of under-
standing of the prevailing mood and viewpoint of the
people of Nova Scotia, who saw confederation not as a
partnership of equals but as subjugation to Canada. Towards the end of his pamphlet Howe wrote: "Instead of
wasting precious time with schemes to dismember the
empire, I wish the Government and people of England
would seriously consider how it can be organized so as to
draw around the throne its vast intellectual and physical
resources . . ."

A few days later, perhaps as a result of these words,
he received a note from Earl Russell asking him to prepare an updated version of his 1854 paper on the organization of the empire. Howe complied in remarkably short
order with an 8,000-word document which again proposed that representatives of the colonies having responsible government should sit in the British parliament,
and that the colonies should contribute men and money
for imperial defence. What this would have meant in
terms of Canada's search for identity and in terms of
world events in the century to come it is difficult to say
and idle to speculate. Earl Russell's power was already in
eclipse and Joe Howe was flying in the face of history.

Chapter 12 "I Can Now Sleep Soundly"

Which colonies became the first provinces of the new Dominion of Canada?

Queen Victoria signed the British North America Act on 27 March, 1867, and 1 July of that year Nova Scotia became part of the new Canada. Since it was obvious that Joe Howe was one of those who should watch over the province's interests in the new parliament, some of his anti-confederate colleagues intimated that they would be satisfied if he now abandoned the struggle and considered his own future. He replied: "Having done my best, I can now sleep soundly." But Howe believed that to have entered the union without consulting the people was a betrayal and a thwarting of the popular wish. In a speech at Dartmouth, scene of bloody Micmac raids in pioneer days, he referred to "The Indians who scalped your forefathers." They had reason for what they did, he said. They were fighting for their country and they were true to it and to each other. They were guilty of no treachery such as that now perpetrated, and ". . . when the last of the Micmacs . . . resigns his soul to his creator, he may look back with pride upon the past, and thank the 'Great Spirit' that there was not a Tupper . . . in his tribe."

With elections in the offing he had a chance to prove his point that entry into confederation was against the will of the people. And prove it he did. In the provincial election, only two supporters of confederation were returned in a House of 38, while only one county returned declared confederates to the first parliament of Canada. On the basis of this, Howe, himself elected by a wide margin, decided to fight for repeal. He carried this fight to London, hoping that if support for his cause could be maintained for six months, the Liberals in England might win power and bring about repeal. Tupper, meanwhile, was also in England. He was confident of victory, but he was shrewd enough to want Joe Howe on his side when the smoke of battle cleared. "He thinks the Canadians will offer us any terms," wrote Howe after Tupper had

visited him," and that he and I combined might rule the
Dominion. Of course I gave him no satisfaction."

Her family now grown up, Susan Ann went with her
husband on this trip. The diary she kept shows little
imaginative flair but it gives interesting glimpses into
their domestic life, and clearly demonstrates the enduring
strength of their attachment. We get, too, the first in-
timations that Howe's health was beginning to fail.

2 April: Joseph's eyes troublesome. I read Dickson's New
        America to him. A very clever book.
3 April: Joseph's eyes very sore.
5 April: In the evening read from the Times Gladstone's speech
        to Joseph, whose eyes are very weak.
22 April: Joseph not well.

Susan Ann Howe in later life

Moving in "high society," they must have had a difficult and anxious time, with the spectre of debt never
far away. "24 April: . . . . Dined and had a bottle of ale and
paid 7/8d. . . . Joseph thought it dear. And we found the
new vegetables was charged extra." Susan Ann, luckily,
was never one for putting on airs, and we find her taking
time out from socializing with the nobility to record:
"25 April: Joseph went to Tattersall's while I washed
some shirts and was busy."

It became increasingly clear that the fight for repeal
was lost, although many would refuse to accept the fact
for a long time. Howe's faith in British politicians was
severely shaken by the Commons debate at which the
fate of Nova Scotia was decided:

"I used to believe that, in a case involving vested interests, constitutional principles, and great sums of money, British statesmen
and legislators would do justice, though the Heavens should fall.
As I strolled home, with deep sorrow, and with a sense of humili-
ation not easily described, I was compelled to acknowledge that
I had cherished a delusion. Anybody else might try a third
experiment, and they shall have all the honour and glory if they
succeed; but I have too much respect for myself, and for my
country, to go a third time begging for justice where none is to be
obtained."

Instead, he returned home and set about getting the
best terms he could for Nova Scotia within Confederation. One thing the delegation had obtained was the
promise of a re-examination of Canadian taxation, trade
and fisheries policies as they would affect Nova Scotia.
Sir John A. Macdonald, prime minister of Canada, was to
come to Halifax in August 1868 to discuss these matters,
but Howe's party — lately so victorious and so strong —

Howe in later life

was torn apart between those who talked irresponsibly of armed resistance and those who wanted annexation to the United States. Howe, so recently the leader in the fight, now spoke out for sanity and moderation, and sought to hold the more hotheaded of his followers in check. Those who spoke of offering open insult to the visiting Canadians, of taking power by seizing government offices, of resisting the law by violent means, were perhaps counting on Joe Howe's leadership. But, said Howe, "I had thought over all these modes of dealing with our difficulties time and again. My reason condemned them, and I was determined that, if lives were to be lost and property wasted, those who favoured such movements should take the lead."

Following the Halifax meetings, which were inconclusive, Howe in a series of letters to Sir John A. Macdonald gradually hammered out a deal Nova Scotians could accept. He maintained his anti-confederate stance, however, so long at is was to Nova Scotia's advantage. "The independence of my position," he wrote to the prime minister, "enables me to fight this battle and I must hold it or be beaten." The battle now was with his own former followers. His influence over them would be gone once he accepted office in the Dominion government. "Looking to the future," he went on, "I must fight my battles here in my own way, and it will be sound policy for you to allay the discontent as fast as you honourably can."

Very largely as a result of Howe's efforts, Macdonald's government went to some lengths to "allay the discontent." By the end of January 1869, negotiations had progressed to a point where Howe felt that he could with good conscience accept office under Macdonald, that he could better serve Nova Scotia from within the government than by harassing it from without. He entered the cabinet as President of the Council.

That winter Howe fought a by-election. He was not one to spare himself, and the long campaign, with day after day of gruelling travel and hour after hour on draughty hustings, left him prostrate for several weeks. But he was hardly up and about before he was off on a jaunt to the Red River district. The prime minister had offered him the post of Secretary of State for the Provinces, and Howe wanted to feel for himself the pulse of

the territory that was to become the new province of
Manitoba. Howe found considerable apprehension
among all sections of the community, but no hostility
that would have led him to anticipate violence if a little
tact and diplomacy were exercised. Yet only a few days
later the new lieutenant-governor, William McDougall,
was intercepted at the border by a party of Métis under
Louis Riel and refused entry. Riel then went on to cap-
ture Fort Garry and establish his own provisional government. When parliament met early in 1870, McDougall
charged that Howe's anti-confederate attitude and in-
discreet talk had contributed to the insurrection. But
there were reliable witnesses to affirm that Howe's conduct during the visit had been scrupulously correct. Not
only was Howe vindicated, but he was able to show that
McDougall's own bungling had helped to provoke the
disorder.

What are Métis?
What do you know about
Louis Riel?
What were the underlying
causes of the unrest?

Although his health had been failing steadily since
the exhausting campaign of 1869, Joe Howe could still
upon occasion work harder than most men, could still
write voluminously, and could still speak with undiminished eloquence whenever there was a cause to be
furthered or an injustice to be exposed. By 1872, however,
illness impaired more and more his ability to fight the
battles he still saw before him. His words lost none of
their forcefulness but a note of sad resignation was
creeping in. There had been many disappointments in
his life and some of his greatest labours had come to
nothing. The most profound disappointment of all,
brought home to him slowly by the succession of events
over a period of years, was the failure of Britain to live
up to the image inspired in him by his father's fierce
unquestioning loyalty. All his proposals for the consol-
idation of the British family had been ignored, and with
the conclusion of the Washington Treaty in 1871, it
finally became clear to him that "both parties in England
would throw us over and buy their peace at our expense, as the Russian woman flings her children to the
wolves. . . ."

How did the Washington
Treaty affect Canada?

For a long time Howe limited his criticism of British
policy to private letters to the governor-general and
others, but in February 1872, in the midst of an other-
wise harmless speech to the Ottawa YMCA, he made
remarks on the subject which infuriated Sir John A.

Statue of Joseph Howe in the grounds of Province House, Halifax

Macdonald. "Our brethren within the narrow seas," he said, "have been counselled to adopt a narrow policy — to call home their legions, and leave the outlying Provinces without a show of sympathy or protection." And he referred publicly now to "England's recent diplomatic efforts to win her own peace at the sacrifice of our interests." What particularly angered Sir John was the suggestion that he had secretly approved the statements. He was on the point of demanding Howe's resignation, commenting tartly: ". . . although he has outlived his usefulness he has not lost his powers of mischief." This was patently unjust. Howe had never flinched from what needed to be said at the prompting of truth or duty, but one would have to look hard and long among his speeches and writings to find evidence of a desire to make mischief. Misguided he may sometimes have been; but rarely indeed, and only under the most extreme provocation, malicious.

In the summer of 1872, Howe wrote to his constituents that he was recuperating in the United States from a severe illness, but was still too ill to campaign for re-election. If they chose to nominate someone else, he said, he would understand. Their reply was to return him by acclamation.

On 6 May, 1873, to no one's surprise but over the protests of a few die-hard repealers who still thought he had betrayed them, Joseph Howe's appointment as lieutenant-governor of Nova Scotia was announced. For Sir John A. Macdonald it may have been a convenient way of putting Howe beyond further "mischief," but the people of Nova Scotia saw it as an honour well deserved and long overdue. Had Howe been in health, it is not likely that Sir John would thus easily have silenced one whose life had been, to quote his own words, "spent in teaching Governors, and Secretaries of State the science of Colonial Govt."

It was not in Joe Howe's nature to be a mere figurehead. But whatever new dimension he might have brought to the viceregal office his countrymen would never know, for in the small hours of 1 June, only three weeks after taking the oath of office, he died. He was, quite simply, worn out. Controversy did not die with him, but Nova Scotia honoured him in her mourning as she has honoured no man before or since. Great crowds filed past him as he lay in state at Government House. When the funeral procession set forth in all the solemn magnificence his high office demanded, it passed through streets so thronged with mourners that "every tree was occupied." Soldiers all along the route presented arms in succession as the bier went by, and minute guns sent their mournful echoes out to sea.

A flood of eulogy filled the press. One paper lamented "The death of the greatest Nova Scotian," while another spoke of "the regrets of those who during so many years have been aided by him, who never aided him very much . . ." The farmers, the same writer commented, "driving along the country roads will stop to talk over his life and tell anecdotes of his conflicts. The tiller of the soil, driving afield, will have his mind full of the strangeness that comes over one on hearing of the death of a great familiar man."

History did not perhaps afford Joe Howe the scope to reveal the true measure of his greatness but in the province of his birth that greatness has been perceived with increasing clarity by succeeding generations. Annually since the centennial of his death, Nova Scotia has celebrated the Joseph Howe Festival: for although the responsible government he helped to win has been swallowed up into something larger; although the intercolonial railway he so selflessly fought for was to be built at last by others; and although the confederation into which Nova Scotia was dragged kicking has turned out to be after all not such a bad thing, plain Joe Howe has been singled out, by that infallible instinct of the people for true heroes, as the man who most nearly symbolizes the spirit of Nova Scotia.

Government House, Halifax, where Howe lived very briefly as Lieutenant-Governor of Nova Scotia, and where he died in 1873

Shortly after Joseph Howe's death, destiny added one last wry touch to the story of the long rivalry between Howe and J. W. Johnston. Johnston was appointed to succeed his old adversary as lieutenant-governor, but died before he could be sworn into office.

Further Reading

Beck, J. Murray. *Joseph Howe: Voice of Nova Scotia*. Toronto: McClelland & Stewart, 1964.

Blakeley, Phyllis R. *Nova Scotia: A Brief History*. Toronto: J. M. Dent, 1955.

Bourinot, Sir John G. *Builders of Nova Scotia*. Toronto: Copp-Clark, 1900.

Fergusson, C. Bruce. *Joseph Howe of Nova Scotia*. Windsor, N.S.: Lancelot Press, 1973.

Howe, Joseph. *Poems and Essays*. Montreal: John Lovell, 1874.

——————— .*Western and Eastern Rambles*. (ed.) M. G. Parks. Toronto: University of Toronto Press, 1973.

Longley, James Wilberforce. *Joseph Howe* ("Makers of Canada" Series). Toronto: Morang, 1911.

Rawlyk, George A. *Joseph Howe: Opportunist? Man of Vision? Frustrated Politician?* Toronto: Copp Clark, 1967.

Roy, James A. *Joseph Howe: A Study in Achievement and Frustration*. Toronto: Macmillan, 1935.

Credits

The author wishes to acknowledge the kindness and unstinting assistance of the staff of the Public Archives of Nova Scotia, and of Murray Barnard of the Nova Scotia Communications and Information Centre.

The publishers wish to express their gratitude to the following who have given permission to use copyrighted illustrations in this book:

Mika Publishing Company, Belleville, Ontario, pages 39, 43

Nova Scotia Communications and Information Centre, pages 33, 34, 35, 36, 50, 51, 60, 61

H. R. Percy, page 14

Public Archives of Nova Scotia, title page, pages 1, 2, 6, 8, 9, 11, 13, 14, 15, 16, 26, 29, 30, 31, 37, 46, 48, 49, 57, 58

Editing: Laura Damania
Design: Jack Steiner
Cover Illustration: Merle Smith

The Canadians

Consulting Editor: Roderick Stewart
Editor-in-Chief: Robert Read

Every effort has been made to credit all sources correctly. The author and publishers will welcome any information that will allow them to correct any errors or omissions.